J.C. Watts Jr.

Community
BUILDERS

J.C. Watts Jr.

Character Counts

by Sarah
De Capua

Children's Press®
A Division of Grolier Publishing
New York London Hong Kong Sydney
Danbury, Connecticut

Photo Credits

Photographs ©: AP/Wide World Photos: 19 (Chuck Burton), 28 (Jerry Laizure); Bob Knudsen: 30; Copyright 1976, Oklahoma Publishing Company: 13 right (From the Aug. 2, 1988 issue of *The Daily Oklahoman.*), 13 left (From the Feb. 3, 1976 issue of *The Daily Oklahoman.*), 23 (From the Nov. 28, 1993 issue of *The Daily Oklahoman.*), 27 (From the Oct. 5, 1994 issue of *The Daily Oklahoman.*); Globe Photos: 8, 35, 44 (James M. Kelly); J.E. Sokolowski: 16; Metro Dade County Department of Tourism: 14; Monkmeyer Press: 9 (Conklin), 6 (Kagan), 37 (Sidney); Office of J.C. Watts, Jr. U.S. House of Representatives: 33, 34, 2.

Reading Consultant
Linda Cornwell, Learning Resource Consultant
Indiana Department of Education

Visit Children's Press on the Internet at:
http://publishing.grolier.com

Library of Congress Cataloging-in-Publication Data

De Capua, Sarah.
    J.C. Watts, Jr.: character counts / by Sarah De Capua.
        p. cm. — (Community builders)
    Includes bibliographical references and index.
    Summary: A biography of the African-American who began life in a poor, black neighborhood in Eufaula, Oklahoma, in 1957, and went on to become a United States congressman.
    ISBN: 0-516-21130-7 (lib. bdg.)   0-516-26346-3 (pbk.)
    1. Watts, J. C. (Julius Caesar), 1957–   . 2. Afro-American legislators—Biography. 3. Legislators—United States—Biography. 4. United States. Congress. House—Biography. 5. Afro-Americans—Politics and government. [1. Watts, J. C. (Julius Caesar), 1957–   . 2. Afro-American legislators. 3. Legislators. 4. Afro-Americans—Biography.] I. Title. II. Series.
E840.8.W39D4 1998
976.6'00496073'0092—dc21
[B]   97-50394
                                                                                                       CIP
                                                                                                        AC

Contents

It can be tempting to steal items that can be
hidden easily inside a pocket.

Chapter ONE

What is Character?

Have you ever thought about stealing a candy bar or a pack of gum from a store because no one was looking? Have you ever been tempted to copy an answer from your classmate's test because your teacher's back was turned? What happened? Did you steal the candy or cheat on the test? If you did, how did you feel about it later?

Sometimes we are faced with difficult choices. It can be hard to be honest. Stealing or cheating can seem easy, but both of these things are wrong. Whether you choose to do something that is wrong says a lot about your character. "Character" means

J. C. Watts Jr.

what kind of person you are. If someone decides not to steal, other people say that the person has good character.

A man who knows all about character is J. C. Watts Jr. Watts has his own special definition for character. He says, "Character is doing what's right when nobody's looking." Watts means that character is knowing the difference between right and wrong, or honesty and dishonesty. Another part of character is choosing to do the right thing—even when you're by yourself.

J. C. Watts Jr. is a United States congressman from Oklahoma. He was first elected to Congress in 1994. Congress is the law-making branch of our country's government. It is located in Washington, D.C., the nation's capital. The Congress is made up

8

A 1996 meeting of the United States Congress

of two parts: the Senate and the House of Representatives. J. C. Watts Jr. serves in the House of Representatives. He was elected by the people who live in the 4th District of Oklahoma. One of the reasons Watts was elected to Congress is that people believe he has good character.

Growing Up in Eufaula

Julius Caesar Watts Jr. was born on November 18, 1957, in the small town of Eufaula, Oklahoma. His family decided to call him "J.C." He is the fifth of six children born to Helen and Buddy Watts. In Eufaula, says Watts, "I grew up in a poor, black neighborhood on the east side of the railroad tracks." The Watts family never had much money, but Watts's parents had dreams of success for all of their children. Helen and Buddy were strict parents, but the Watts children never doubted how much their parents loved them.

Oklahoma

With more three million inhabitants, the state of Oklahoma is located in the Great Plains. Oklahoma's two largest cities are Oklahoma City (the state capital) and Tulsa. J. C. Watts Jr.'s hometown of Eufaula lies about 60 miles (97 kilometers) southeast of Tulsa.

Important products from Oklahoma include beef cattle, cotton, dairy products, machinery, aircraft, electronics, and more. The state is also rich in natural resources such as water, soil, forests, coal, minerals, natural gas, and petroleum (oil).

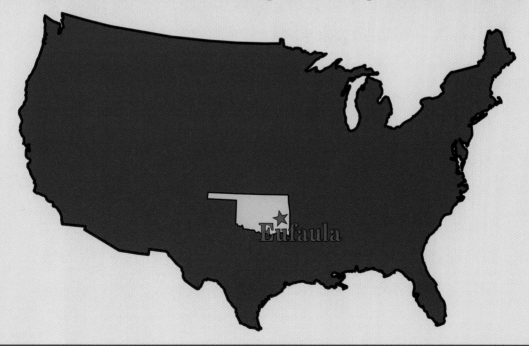

Eufaula

Despite being poor, Helen and Buddy Watts had a strong belief in education. They encouraged J.C. and his brothers and sisters to work hard at their studies. Watts credits his mom and dad with teaching him something more important than hard work, however: values. Values are beliefs and ideas about what is most important in a person's life. So J.C. Watts Jr. learned to be honest and to keep his word. He learned to admit he was wrong when he made mistakes. "My parents taught me and my brothers and sisters that if you make a mistake, you've got to own up to it, and then try to turn it around [so you don't make the same mistake again]."

J.C. Watts Jr. also learned to find creative ways to solve problems. He learned to care about others and to spend time helping them. He also learned that he could do anything he wanted if he applied himself and stuck with it. Today, J.C. Watts Jr. is still grateful for the values and strong character his parents helped him to develop.

Watts graduated from Eufaula High School in 1976. He then attended the University of Oklahoma

12

J.C. Watts Jr. (left) in 1976, the year he graduated from high school. By 1979, Watts (right) was a football star at the University of Oklahoma.

and graduated in 1981. While at the University of Oklahoma, he became well known as the quarterback for the Oklahoma Sooners football team. He led the team to two conference championships. (A conference is a group of athletic teams in a certain region.) He also led the Sooners to victories in the 1980 and 1981 Orange Bowl.

13

The Orange Bowl

At the end of each college football season, the teams with the best records are invited to play in "bowl games." Most bowl games are played in late December or on January 1. One of these bowl games is the Orange Bowl. It was established in 1935 and is played each year in Miami, Florida.

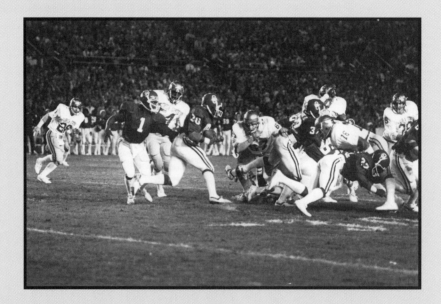

Watts (# 1) and the Oklahoma Sooners played against the Florida State Seminoles in the 1980 Orange Bowl.

Watts, with the award he received at his 1992 induction to the Orange Bowl Hall of Honor

As a result of J. C. Watts's leadership on the football field, he was named the team's Most Valuable Player (MVP) after both Orange Bowl wins. Later, in 1992, he was inducted into the Orange Bowl Hall of Honor, which is reserved for the best players ever to participate in the Orange Bowl.

Watts in 1983, while playing for the Toronto Argonauts professional football team

After Watts graduated from the University of Oklahoma, he spent six years in Canada starring in the Canadian Football League. He played first for the Ottawa Rough Riders, then for the Toronto Argonauts. In 1983, Watts was voted the MVP of the Grey Cup—the Canadian Football League's "Super Bowl."

16

Hard Work . . . and History

After leaving the Canadian Football League, Watts, his wife Frankie, and their children returned to Oklahoma in January 1987. They settled in Norman, a city of about 80,000 people that is located 25 miles (40 km) south of Oklahoma City, the state capital.

In Norman, J.C. Watts Jr. worked in real estate and petroleum marketing. Watts became the owner of a property management company. Property man-

**Frankie Watts, with three of the Watts children
(from left): Trey, Julie, and Jennifer**

agement companies collect homeowners' dues, and
provide maintenance and repairs. In addition to
owning his own company, Watts took a job as the
youth minister at Sunnylane Southern Baptist
Church in Del City, Oklahoma. To minister means to

18

help or to serve someone. As a youth minister, Watts served as a spiritual and moral guide for young people. He encouraged them to have faith and to turn to their religion when they have problems. Watts found this work rewarding. He especially enjoyed working with disadvantaged, or low-income, youths. Watts remembered what it was like to grow up poor. He also remembered how important it was to have

J. C. Watts Jr. brings his talent for speaking to young people to many situations. Here, he talks to a group of high school students in Charlotte, North Carolina, in November 1997.

loving parents who set good examples for him. He wanted to spread the lessons his parents taught him. So J. C. Watts Jr. set out to be a good role model for the young people in his youth group. He had a unique way of talking with them. He treated them all with respect. He listened to their problems, and helped them find solutions. Most of all, he made them feel special. Sometimes it was hard work to be

The Watts Children

J. C. and Frankie Watts have five children: Keisha, Jerrelle, Jennifer, Trey, and Julie. J. C.'s oldest daughter serves in the United States Air Force. The younger children keep J. C. and Frankie busy at the park near their home—playing on swings and running around the merry-go-round.

involved in the lives of so many people. He and Frankie already had five children to raise. But J. C. Watts Jr. liked the hard work and the positive influence he had on their lives.

During the next few years, Watts's reputation as an honest, hardworking leader in his community grew steadily. Many people, adults as well as young people, felt great respect for Watts because he was outspoken about the things that mattered to the people where he lived: family, education, hard work, faith, and compassion. Some people thought so much of J. C. Watts's leadership abilities that they began to encourage him to run for elective office. Watts, too, believed this was a good idea.

In 1990, Watts ran for the office of Oklahoma Corporation Commissioner. The Corporation Commission makes the rules for the state's energy industry. It ensures that people are offered fair prices for oil and gas. The commission also works to be sure that no energy company makes too much more money than another energy company. Since Oklahoma is one of the United States's largest oil-

Workers on an oil rig in Oklahoma

and gas-producing states, the job of corporation commissioner is an important one. It requires someone who is honest and dedicated to following the law.

J. C. Watts Jr. believed he was the right person for the job. The voters of Oklahoma agreed with him. Watts won the election and became the state's commissioner, a job that usually lasts for four years. It was an important step in J. C. Watts Jr.'s life because it meant that the voters trusted him.

However, Watts's victory was meaningful for another reason: It made him the first black person to be elected to statewide office in Oklahoma history.

J. C. Watts Jr. listens to members at a 1993 meeting of the Oklahoma Corporation Commission.

From Oklahoma to Washington, D.C.

As Oklahoma's corporation commissioner, J. C. Watts Jr. became even more well known in his home state. The more people got to know him, the more they liked and respected him. Despite his busy job as corporation commissioner, Watts still found time to continue his youth ministry work. At the same time, Watts considered his wife and children to be his most important responsibility. But one of the things the people liked most of all was the way Watts spoke out against drugs and alcohol. He told students that using drugs and alcohol would ruin their character. He also told them to stay in school. He encouraged them to work hard, to be honest, and

24

to be dedicated to becoming good people who care about others.

As J.C. Watts Jr. continued his work, he began to consider running in another election. This election, though, was a position even higher than state corporation commissioner. It was for the honor of serving in the United States Congress as an Oklahoma state representative. If Watts won the election, he would go to Washington, D.C., and serve in the House of Representatives. He would represent the people of

District

A district is an area or a region that is set up within a state. Most of the states in the United States are divided into districts. When congressional elections are held, people in each district vote for the person they believe will speak for them in Washington, D.C.

While speaking to reporters during his campaign for Congress, Watts is joined here by Congressman Newt Gingrich of Georgia.

This photograph, which appeared in *The Daily Oklahoman* newspaper, shows J. C. Watts Jr. and other candidates for Congress addressing the issues that were important to voters.

Oklahoma's 4th congressional district. There are only six people who are allowed to represent the citizens of Oklahoma in the House of Representatives. J. C. Watts Jr. wanted to be one of them. He believed he had good ideas about how to improve people's lives.

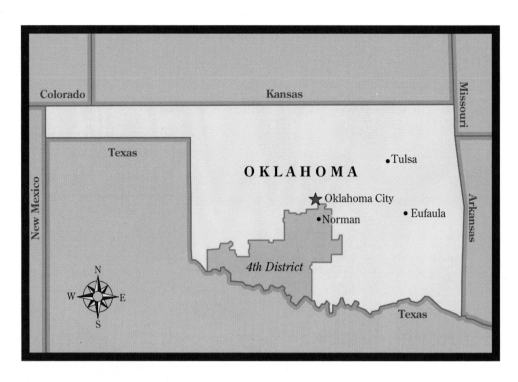

Oklahoma's 4th congressional district is located
in the southwestern part of the state.

Watts entered the 1994 race to succeed a state
representative named Dave McCurdy. Watts was in
the race as a Republican. (There are two main polit-
ical parties in the United States: the Republicans
and the Democrats.) There were four other men
running against J. C. Watts Jr. as Republicans, too.
But Watts had an advantage because the voters of
the 4th District already knew him. They respected

28

him. Watts had a good reputation as a leader, and the people supported him.

In the November election, more than half of the voters in Oklahoma's 4th congressional district voted for J.C. Watts Jr. Once again, Watts had won an important election. J.C. Watts Jr.'s election to the United States Congress wasn't just an honor for him, however. His election made history. It marked the first time since Reconstruction that a southern state elected a black Republican to Congress.

Reconstruction

Reconstruction (1865–77) was a period in the United States that followed the Civil War (1861–65). The war left the South devastated. During Reconstruction, the Northern and Southern states reunified. Also during this time, the South rebuilt its railroads, farms, industries, and factories.

U.S. Representative J. C. Watts Jr. in his
congressional office in the Capitol

Chapter FIVE

Making a Difference

J.C. Watts Jr. began his two-year term of office in the House of Representatives in January 1995. Immediately, he set to work bringing more attention to the things that matter most to him: families and communities.

Together with two other representatives, Watts introduced a bill called the American Community Renewal Act. The bill is the result of work and research that took eight years to complete. It is a three-step plan to improve poor communities throughout the United States.

American Community Renewal

The American Community Renewal Act has three major themes:

1. Finding ways to strengthen families

2. Getting jobs for out-of-work community members

3. Improving education opportunities for all of the members of a community, especially the children

Watts believes strongly in the American Community Renewal Act because it focuses on the power of people. "I have faith in the American people," says Watts. "This act reflects American ideals by helping individuals renew their communities through the values of faith, family, work, neighborhood, and community." J. C. Watts Jr. believes that people have the power to work together to make great changes in their communities.

Representative J. C. Watts Jr. has become well known in Congress for other important work, as well. He is a member of several Congressional committees, including a committee that studies solutions to minority issues and concerns. Watts was

Watts visits with children on the steps of a community center during a Community Renewal tour.

Watts (right), with dedicated assistants and Congressional workers

given a special place on a committee that studies housing problems because its members were anxious to hear his opinions and ideas. Watts is also active in national organizations called the Orphan Foundation of America (OFA) and the March of Dimes. The OFA provides love and support to children who are growing up without parents. The March of Dimes is dedicated to improving the health of babies by reducing birth defects and infant deaths.

Perhaps J. C. Watts Jr.'s most important work, however, is with children and teenagers. In addition to his work in Congress, Watts has served as associate pastor of Sunnylane Southern Baptist Church in

**Representative Watts awaits his turn to speak during
a 1997 meeting of the Congressional committee
on education and the workforce.**

Del City, Oklahoma, since 1995. Also in 1995, Watts became the spokesman for the Fellowship of Christian Athletes. He is also the spokesman for various anti-drug campaigns across Oklahoma, as well as the United States. When Watts talks to students about drugs and alcohol, he teaches them about character. He reminds them that "character is doing what's right when nobody's looking." He also shares his important message: "Young people," he

Fellowship of Christian Athletes

The Fellowship of Christian Athletes (FCA) was begun in 1954. The organization can be found at schools and colleges throughout the United States. The FCA uses volunteers to help athletes, coaches, and others deal with everyday problems in their lives.

Watts supports many of the programs that educate children about the dangers of drugs and alcohol.

says, "America needs you. If our country is going to continue to be great . . . [and] strong, you are going to have to do your part. You are going to have to fight . . . against skipping school and cheating on your papers. Fight against disobeying your parents. Fight against cursing and smoking. And fight, fight, fight against drugs and alcohol."

J. C. Watts Jr. (second row, second from left), with the winners and presenters of the 1996 Outstanding Young Americans award

J. C. Watts Jr. has been so successful both in reaching young people, and in serving his congressional community, that Oklahoma's Junior Chamber of Commerce named him one of the Ten Outstanding Young Americans for 1996. Another sign of

Watts's fine service to the people of his district was his reelection to a second two-year term in 1996. (Watts will be eligible to run for a third term in November 1998.)

During the summer of 1996, the Republican Party held its national convention in San Diego, California. There were several important people

Watts addressed the Republican National Convention on August 13, 1996.

As student assistants look on, Watts removes his
microphone after giving the Republican response to
the president's 1997 State of the Union address.

who were invited to address the crowd. Congressman Watts was one of the speakers. It was a special moment for Watts, who said, "In my wildest imagination, I never thought that a child born in a poor, black neighborhood, in a rural community, would someday be called 'congressman.'" Watts said he owes his success to the strong character he learned from his parents.

Early each year, the president of the United States appears before Congress to deliver a speech called the State of the Union address. The speech is carried live throughout the nation on television. Immediately after, a member of Congress gives a response to the president's speech. In February 1997, President Bill Clinton gave the State of the Union address. J.C. Watts Jr. was honored again when he was chosen to respond to Clinton's speech.

In his speech, Watts talked about his love for the United States and for his family. He talked about the things Americans can do to make the country a better place to live. He said, "We must make our mark on the future as a people who care for our families, for one another, for our neighbors, and for all the children. We must be people who share and help each other in need. We must be people who take responsibility for our actions and ask God to heal us."

People throughout the United States watched the congressman on television. Some who didn't already know J. C. Watts Jr. heard him speak that night for the first time. Many people liked what they heard. Some were so impressed that they believe Watts will one day be the first black president of the United States.

Today, Representative Watts continues to be a spokesman for important issues. Watts tells people of all ages to be responsible, caring members of their communities. He believes that personal achievement and racial equality, along with hard work and dedication, are keys to the success of our country. Most of all, J. C. Watts Jr. strives to be an example of good character for others, especially young people, to follow. "Always remember," says Watts, "that character does count."

J. C. Watts Jr. appeared on a national television news program called "Meet the Press" on March 16, 1997. He discussed his views about several issues, including race, education, and character.

In Your Community

J.C. Watts Jr. has many ideas for making communities better places to live. One of his plans is the American Community Renewal Act. One part of the act suggests ways to improve education for people, especially children, in a community. How can you help? Here are some suggestions:

- Many parents of pre-school children don't have enough money to purchase storybooks. Do you have any storybooks, or other

Timeline

Watts graduates from Eufaula High School.

Watts again named MVP of Orange Bowl; graduates from University of Oklahoma.

Watts named MVP of Canada's Grey Cup.

1957 — **1976** — **1980** — **1981** — **1981–1986** — **1983**

J. C. Watts Jr. born in Eufaula, Oklahoma, on November 18.

Watts named MVP of Orange Bowl.

Watts plays in Canadian Football League.

books you've outgrown, that you'd like to donate to these younger children?

- Some school libraries don't have money to buy books, either. Why not donate books you don't read anymore? Perhaps you can organize your friends or classmates to donate, too. Your teacher or school librarian can help you get in touch with communities in need.
- If you don't have books to donate, you may want to volunteer to read storybooks to your school's kindergartners.
- Perhaps a first- or second-grader is having trouble learning to read. Ask an adult if you can be a tutor.

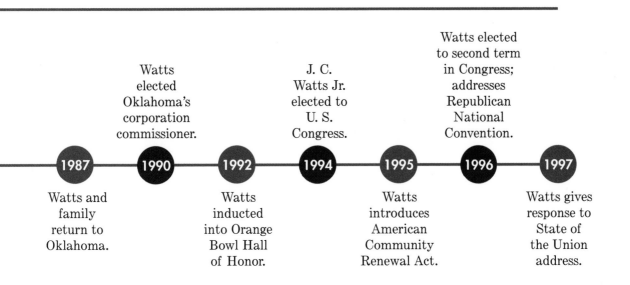

Watts elected Oklahoma's corporation commissioner.

J. C. Watts Jr. elected to U. S. Congress.

Watts elected to second term in Congress; addresses Republican National Convention.

1987 — **1990** — **1992** — **1994** — **1995** — **1996** — **1997**

Watts and family return to Oklahoma.

Watts inducted into Orange Bowl Hall of Honor.

Watts introduces American Community Renewal Act.

Watts gives response to State of the Union address.

To Find Out More

Here are some additional resources to help you learn more about J. C. Watts Jr., the U.S. Congress, Oklahoma, and more:

Books

Feinberg, Barbara Silberdick.
   Local Governments.
   Franklin Watts, 1993.

Fradin, Dennis B.
   Oklahoma. Children's
   Press, 1995.

Gourse, Leslie.
   The Congress.
   Franklin Watts, 1994.

Stein. R. Conrad.
   The Powers of Congress.
   Children's Press, 1995.

Sutherland, Charles.
   Character for Champions.
   Vantage Press, Inc., 1995.

Organizations and Online Sites

Fellowship of Christian Athletes
8701 Leeds Road
Kansas City, MO 64129
http://www.fca.org

Representative J. C. Watts Jr.
Legislative Office
1210 Longworth House
   Office Building
Washington, DC 20515
*http://www.rep.jcwatts@mail.
house.gov*
Here you'll find a biography of
Watts, a guest book you can sign,
a photo album, information about
Oklahoma's 4th District, and a
list of answers to FAQ's.

Representative J. C. Watts Jr.
District Office
2420 Springer Drive, Suite 120
Norman, OK 73069

Representative J. C. Watts Jr.
District Office
601 S.W. D Avenue, Suite 205
Lawton, OK 73501

Index

About
the Author

Sarah De Capua was born
and raised in Connecticut.
She resides in Danbury, Con-
necticut, where she works as an editor of children's
books, and spends most of her free time playing
with her cocker spaniel, Bailey.

In researching this book, Ms. De Capua enjoyed
learning about Congressman Watts's commitment
to his faith and his family, as well as his dedication to
helping people help themselves. Ms. De Capua is
proud to dedicate this book to her parents, who have
taught by example that character counts.